sketching with Watercolour PENCILS

Written and designed by the Top That!™ team
Illustrated by Gilly Marklew & Peter Wilks

TOP THAT!

Published by Top That! Publishing
Tide Mill Way, Woodbridge,
Suffolk, IP12 1AP, UK
www.topthatpublishing.com
Copyright © 2002 Top That! Publishing plc
Top That! is a Registered Trade Mark of Top That! Publishing plc
All rights reserved

SKETCHING WITH WATERCOLOUR PENCILS

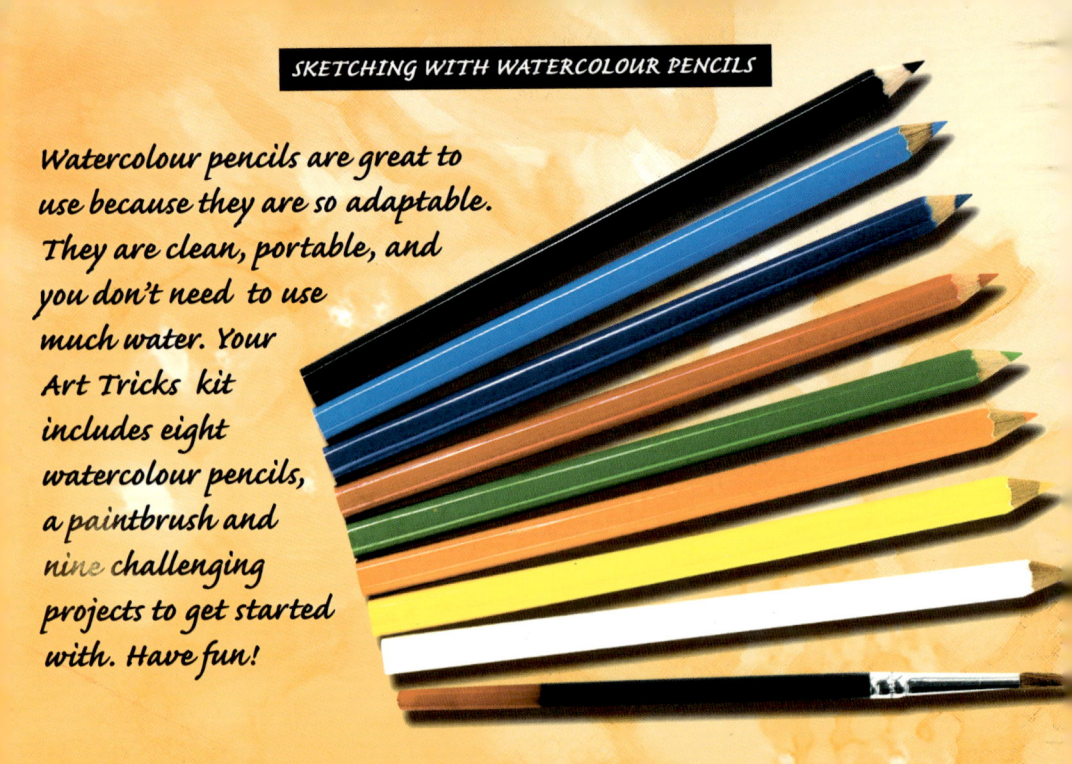

Watercolour pencils are great to use because they are so adaptable. They are clean, portable, and you don't need to use much water. Your Art Tricks kit includes eight watercolour pencils, a paintbrush and nine challenging projects to get started with. Have fun!

Using Watercolour Pencils

Watercolour pencils soften and dissolve on contact with water. Try the following techniques to get used to them.

1. Draw with pencils, then brush over with a wet paintbrush to spread colour. This technique is ideal for colouring in large areas.

2. Wet the end of your pencil and then draw to create bold strokes of colour.

3. Use dry watercolour pencils for drawing in detail as you would a normal coloured pencil.

The possibilities are endless with watercolour pencils. There is no right or wrong way to use them, all you need is your imagination!

SKETCHING WITH WATERCOLOUR PENCILS

There is a practice pad at the back of this book. Use it to practise using your watercolour pencils.

Projects

This book will guide you through the basics of sketching with watercolour pencils. There are nine fun projects for you to complete. Start by tracing the outline at the beginning of each project and then follow the simple steps to learn the key techniques. Look at the finished picture on the final page of each project to see which colours go where.

Extra Items

To complete the projects in this book, there are a few extra items you will need. A pencil sharpener, good quality paper and a jar of water are all essential. Tissues for blotting your brush and a plastic eraser are good to have, too.

Basic Techniques

Before you start the projects, take time to learn the basic skills and techniques of watercolour pencil sketching. The first few pages of this book teach you how to get the most out of your pencils, including how to mix new colours, using the watercolour pencils provided, and making various types of marks with both pencils and your paintbrush. It is important that you get used to using the pencils dry and wet, so that you are able to begin the projects with confidence.

Crosshatching

Crosshatching can be used to vary textures and colours. Simply shade lines of one colour and then draw over the lines in the opposite direction with the same colour, or choose another colour to create a whole new hue.

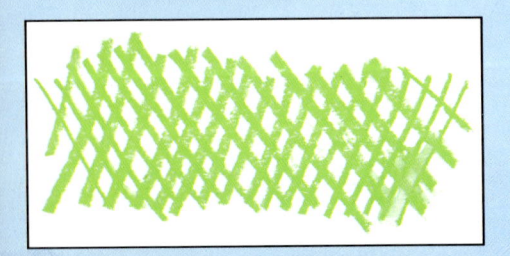

Brushing Out Colour

Convert dry pencil shading into watercolour wash, by lightly brushing over it with clean water.

Use dry pencils and a wet paintbrush to recreate the wash effects shown below.

Light shading, brushed out into washed colour using a wet paintbrush.

Heavy shading, brushed out into washed colour using a wet paintbrush.

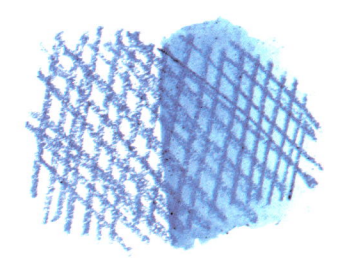

SKETCHING WITH WATERCOLOUR PENCILS

Brush Strokes

Use the brush to mix colours, soften lines and to spread colour on the page. Or, draw onto a palette, add a little water and use the brush to apply the colour directly onto the paper.

Textured washes are made by brushing over fine and coarse crosshatching

Loose stroke marks

Coarse stroke marks

Blotting

Use a damp tissue to remove any unwanted colour from your sketch. This technique is really useful if you want to create backgrounds which fade into the distance.

5

SKETCHING WITH WATERCOLOUR PENCILS

Wet on Dry

Wet the tip of your pencil before sketching to achieve strong lines and shading.

A zig zag of sharp wetted colour.

Texture created by rolling the wetted pencils while you colour.

Dry on Wet

Sketch onto damp paper to achieve fuzzy streaks which are ideal for trees, bushes and backgrounds.

Dry on Dry

Increase colour intensity by applying a second layer over the top of a previously applied colour which has dried. Continue applying additional layers of colour until you achieve the effect you want. Always allow each layer of colour to dry before applying the next.

SKETCHING WITH WATERCOLOUR PENCILS

Grading Your Colour

Background colours are often graded. This means that various shades of a colour range from light to dark. You can achieve a graded effect by sketching your colour onto a piece of paper with a dry watercolour pencil, then with a wet paintbrush, applying water over the colour, gradually spreading it up, as shown (right).

Try grading two different colours, gradually easing the colours together as shown (below).

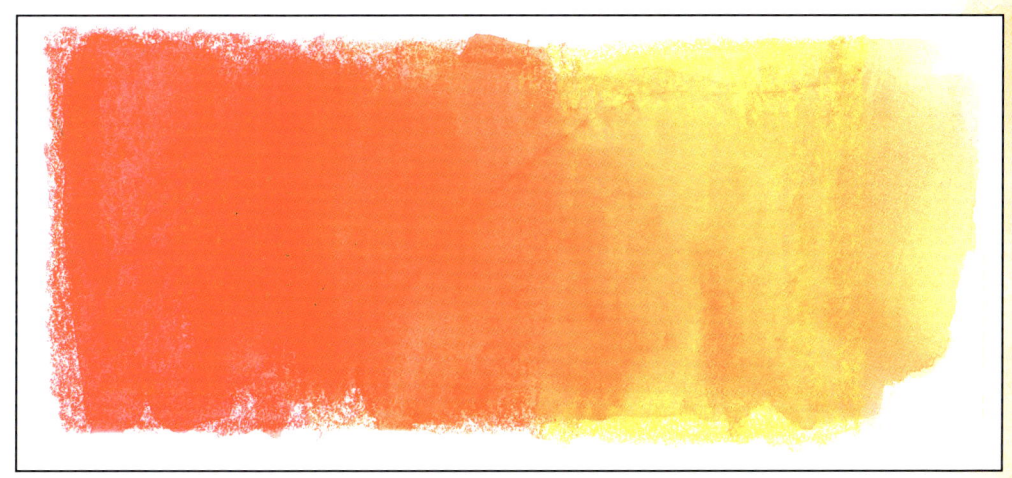

Colour Magic

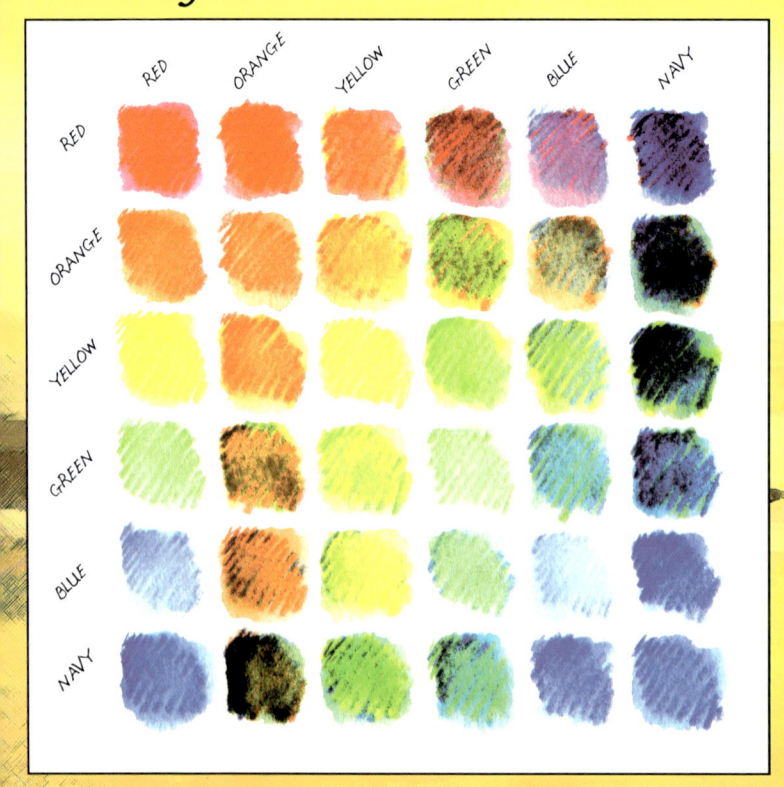

Find the colour you want in the block, then look along its row and column to find the colours you need to mix that colour. Crosshatch the two colours together, then brush out the new colour with clean water and your paintbrush.

By adding different colours to a picture you can change the shape, form and texture. For some of the projects you may not have the right colours.

This colour block shows you which colours you need to mix to make the colour you want.

SKETCHING WITH WATERCOLOUR PENCILS

Each project comes with a colour chart which shows you what colours you need to mix. Experiment with different colour combinations before you start – it may take a while to get the exact colour you want.

Some pencil colours can look a little unnatural. Make them look richer by adding different colours like brown, red or blue as shown (right).

You can weaken colours by adding water or white as pictured (below).

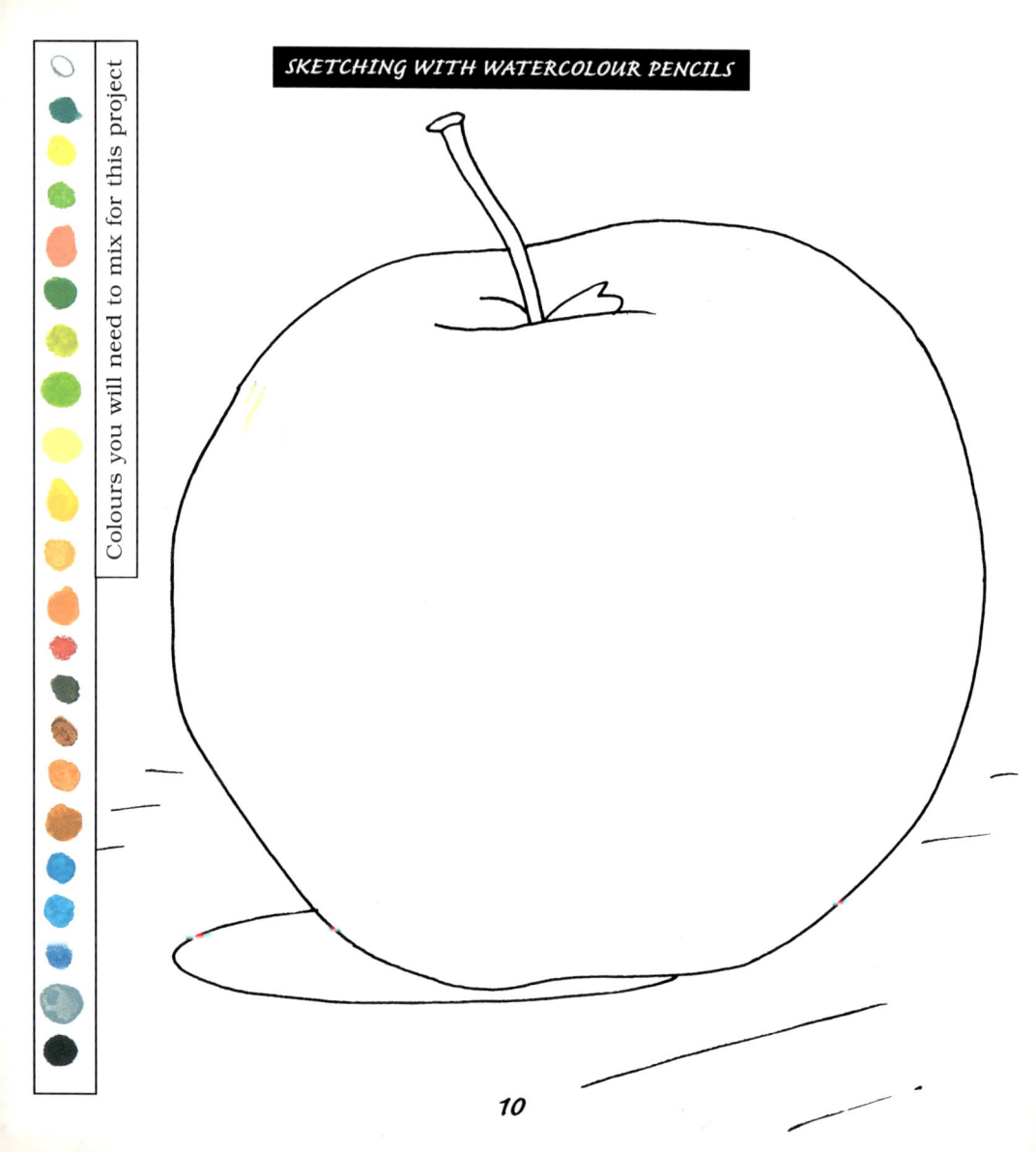

SKETCHING WITH WATERCOLOUR PENCILS

Colours you will need to mix for this project

10

SKETCHING WITH WATERCOLOUR PENCILS

Apple: Light & Shade

1. Start by sketching in the background which ranges from dark to light (see the finished picture on page 13 to see which colours go where). To do this, grade black to blue to grey to white. Dip your paintbrush into clean water and brush over the colours to help blend them together.

2. Draw in the darker brown, green and red colouring on the apple and lighten with water using a brush to dilute the colour. Gradually build up the main body of the apple using a yellow wash which grades to orange.

SKETCHING WITH WATERCOLOUR PENCILS

3. To create a realistic apple texture, use wet red and green pencils, on areas that are still wet, to apply the soft stripes of colour shown (opposite). Use dry watercolour pencils, when the underpainting has dried, to add the details.

4. When colouring areas of the apple that are in shade, make them slightly darker. Define smaller details, such as the stalk, with an additional layer of colour using a sharp, dry pencil.

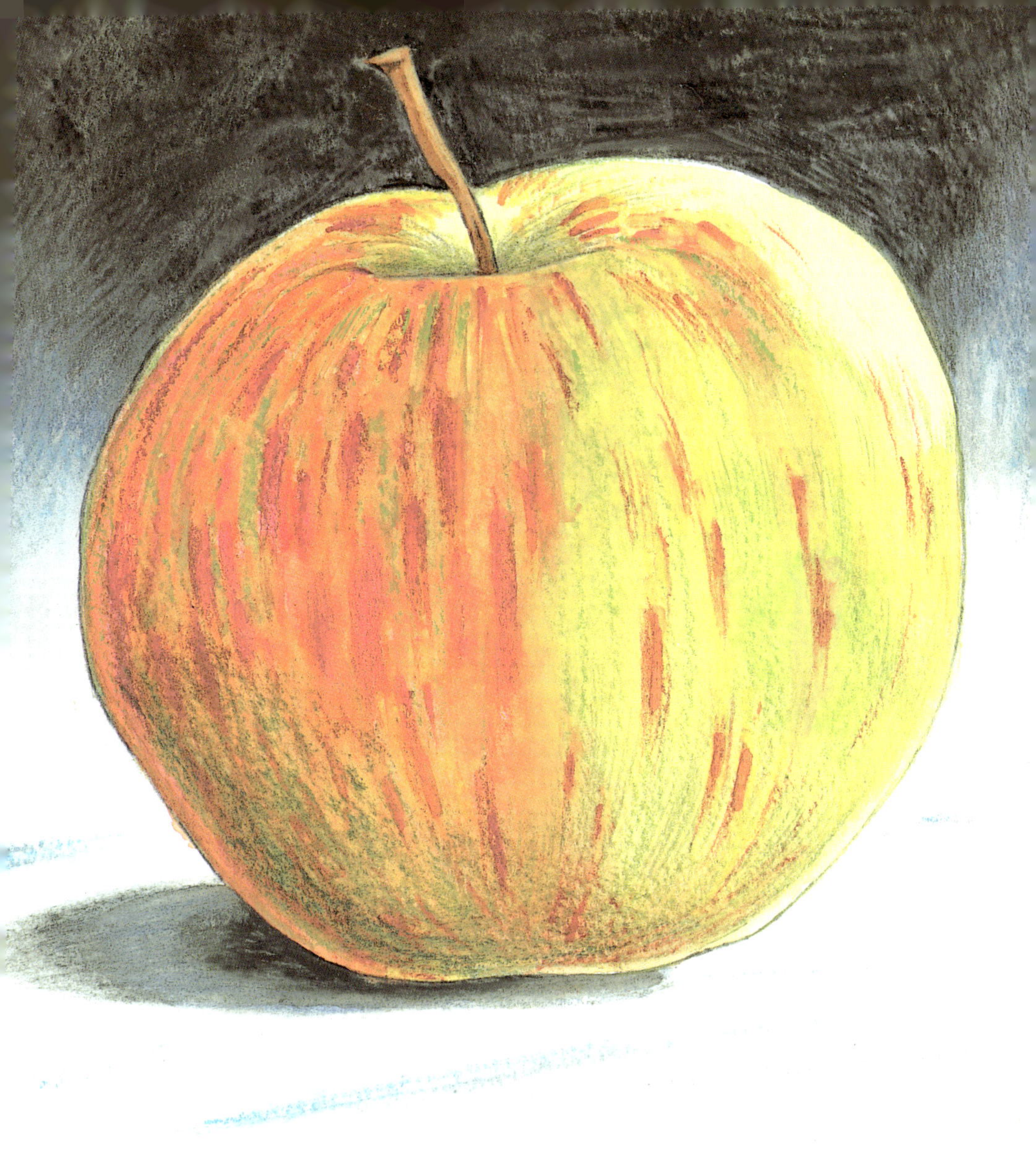

SKETCHING WITH WATERCOLOUR PENCILS

African Desert Plain: Depth

1. To sketch the sky, mix a dry light grey colour for the clouds and light blue for the sky. Brush over the dry colours, in a swirling motion, with a wet brush. Use a dry pencil to add detail, such as shading, to the edge of the clouds, when dry.

Colours you will need to mix for this project

SKETCHING WITH WATERCOLOUR PENCILS

2. Following the colour chart, below, use green and brown to draw the trees. Apply lighter colours first, building up to the darker areas. Use short circular strokes and wet pencils to create the leaves. Use solid line strokes and a wet pencil for the tree trunks. Soften the leaves using a clean, wet brush.

SKETCHING WITH WATERCOLOUR PENCILS

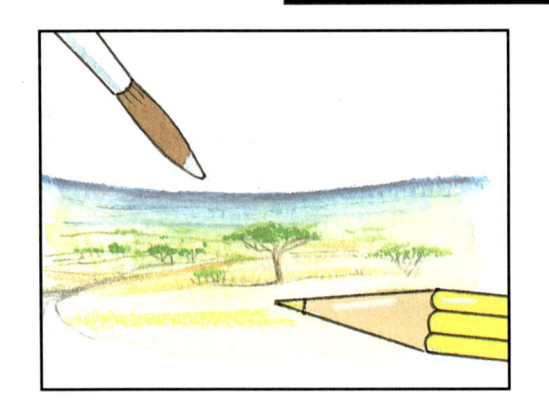

3. *Colour the background, using subtle shades of brown washed over with a wet brush. Grade the blue mountain range by picking up colour from the tips of your pencils onto a paintbrush. To do this, wet the pencil and transfer the colour onto the paintbrush.*

SKETCHING WITH WATERCOLOUR PENCILS

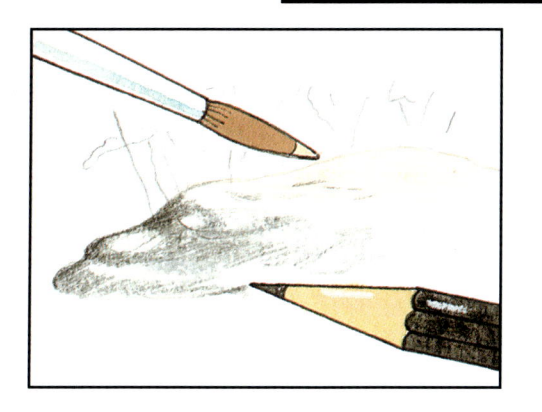

4. Mix a beige colour to cover the rocks, then wash over with a wet brush. Fill in the folds and crevices of the rocks with a grey colour. Finally, draw in green clumps of grass using short line strokes and a combination of wet and dry watercolour pencils.

Colours you will need to mix for this project.

Italian Mountain Scene: Composition

1. Sketch in the sky with a wet, blue watercolour pencil. Leave white spaces where the clouds would be. Use a wet brush to blur the edge of the area where the clouds will be. Using darker blue, fill in the mountain with a wet watercolour pencil. Use a clean wet brush to lighten the base of the mountain.

2. Use wet pencils to fill in the walls, roof, shutters and windows with colours such as beige, brown and grey. Wash over these areas with a wet brush. Take a dry watercolour pencil and draw in all the fine details of the stonework and roof tiles, using the same colours as before.

SKETCHING WITH WATERCOLOUR PENCILS

3. Once the sky has dried, use wet, green watercolour pencils to draw in the foliage. Use a brown mix to fill in the trees using the rolling method (see page 6). Use a light shade first, then gradually build up darker shades. Add all the branches and fine detail with a small brush.

4. Gradually build up the different tones of the background. Start with the fields. With a wet, watercolour pencil and paintbrush, apply light greens and yellows to begin with, then move on to darker shades. Use yellow and orange washes to fill in the houses, then draw in the fine detail of the roofs and windows with a dry, sharp, black pencil.

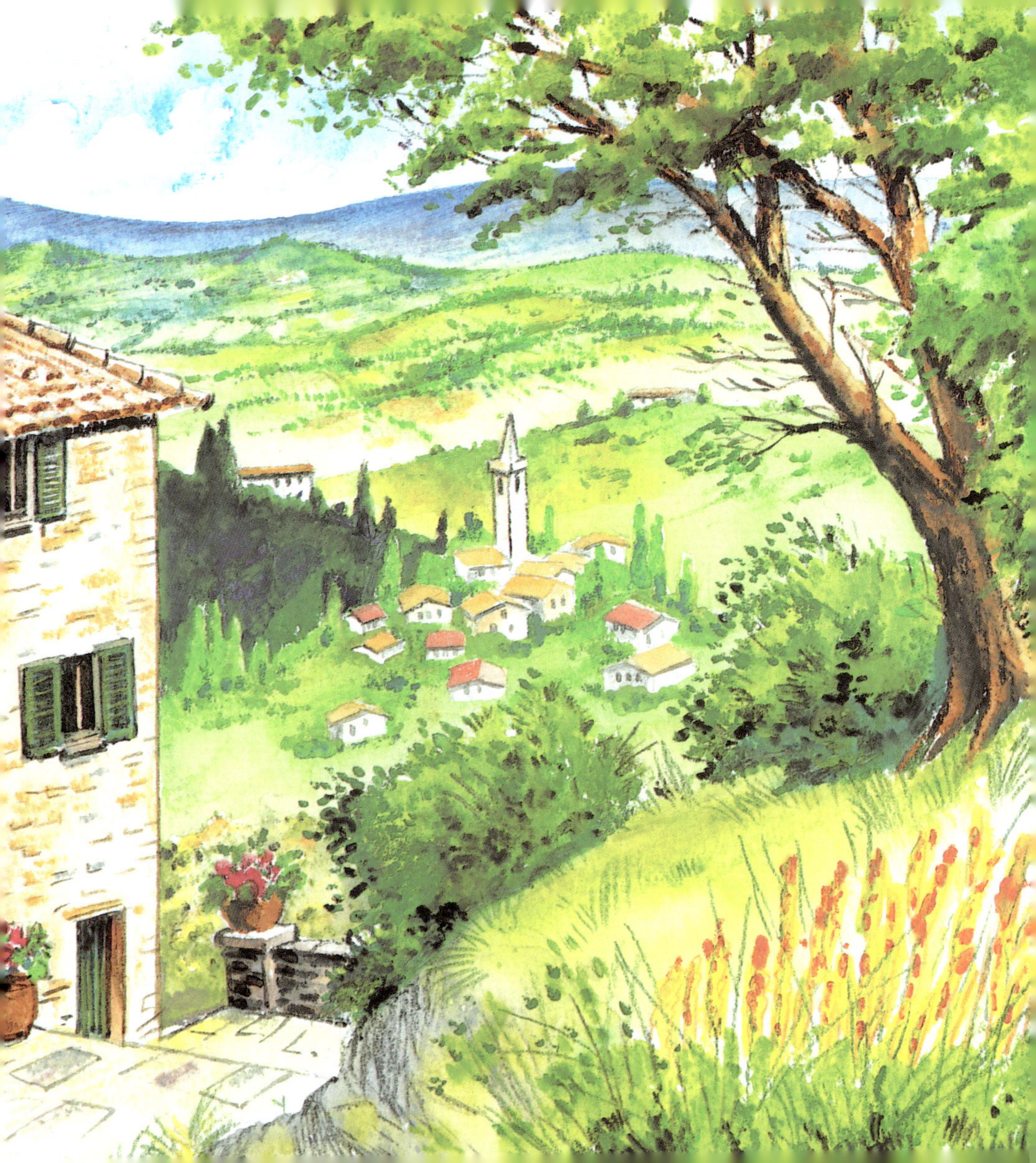

Colours you will need to mix for this project

SKETCHING WITH WATERCOLOUR PENCILS

Brooklyn Street Scene: Perspective

1. Using the colours shown in the finished picture on page 25, shade in the foundation colours of the buildings with wet watercolour pencils. Add the stonework texture with a damp, black watercolour pencil using short strokes.

2. Carefully draw the 'DON'T WALK' lettering on the sign with a pencil, then colour in the letters with a wet, red watercolour pencil. Wet a black pencil and shade around the lettering. Sketch the rest of the sign with a mix of dry orange and white watercolour pencils.

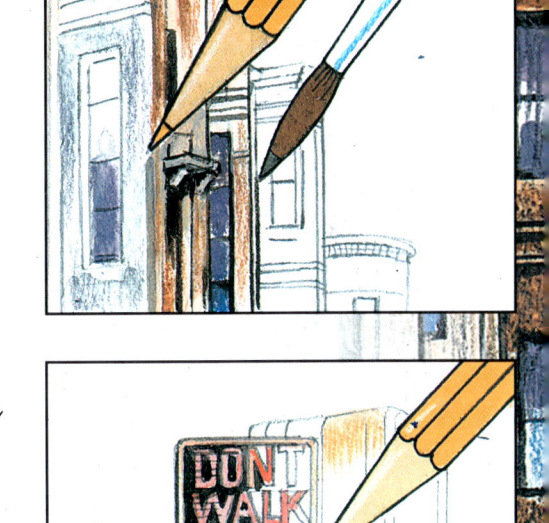

SKETCHING WITH WATERCOLOUR PENCILS

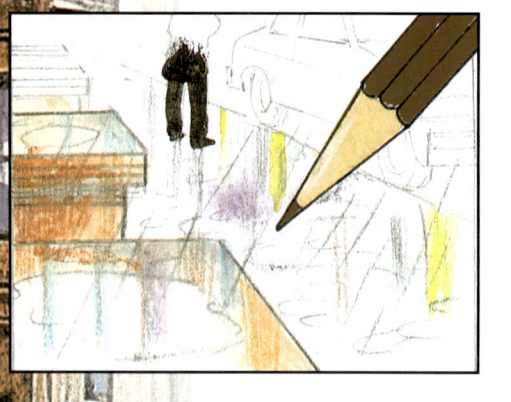

3. Shade in the puddles and people using a mix of grey and black colours. Gradually build up darker colours, then brush over with a wet brush. When dry, use dry pencils to draw feint reflections in the water. Outline the puddles using dry, black, blue and yellow colours as shown (opposite).

4. Roughly sketch in the colours of the sky and distant buildings using grey, purple and blue, wet watercolour pencils. Wash over these areas with a wet brush. Use a black, dry watercolour pencil to add the fine details of the buildings and strokes of rain across the picture. Make sure the thin long strokes for the rain aren't too dark.

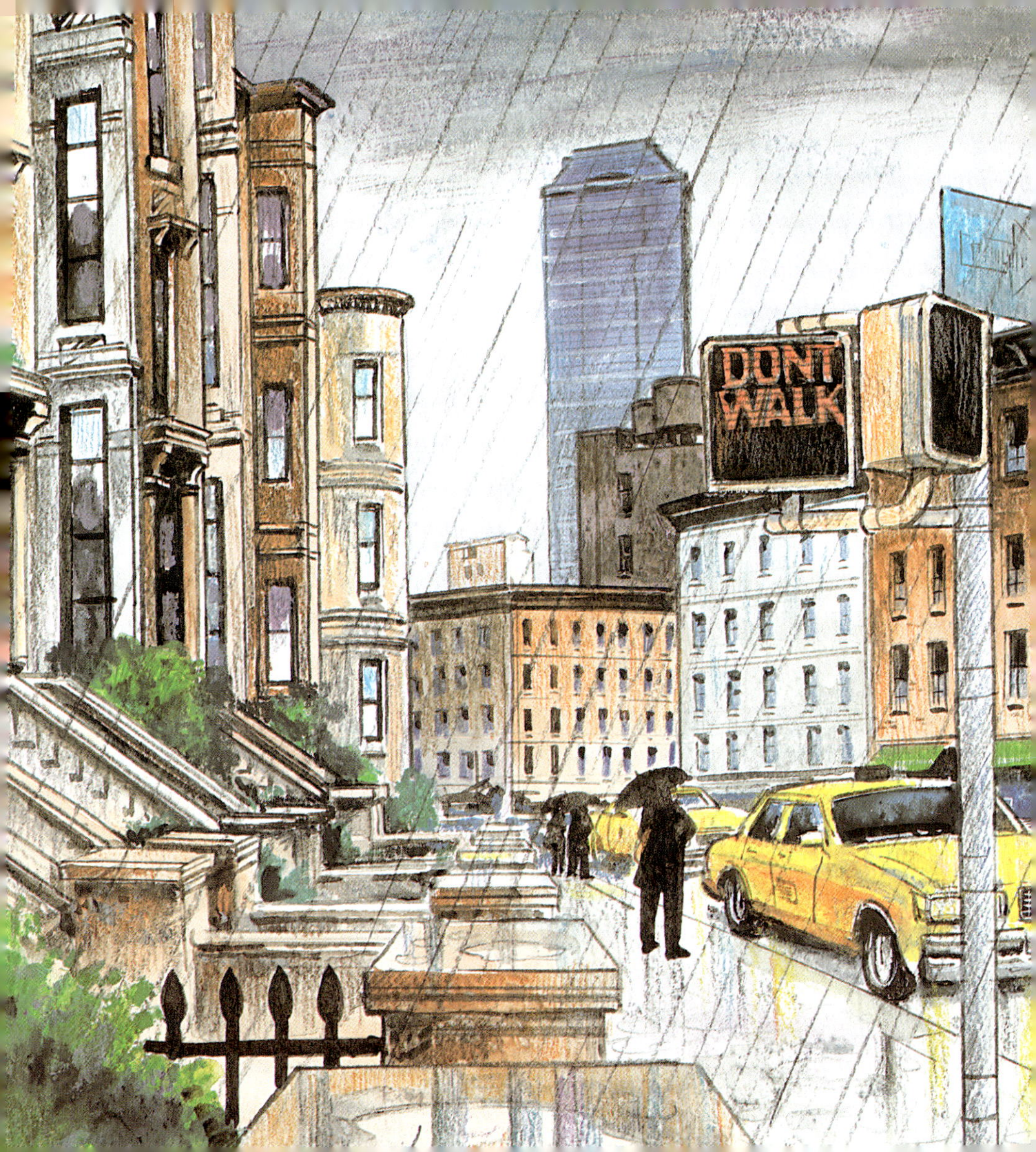
DON'T
WALK

Colours you will need to mix for this project

SKETCHING WITH WATERCOLOUR PENCILS

Tropical Fish: Scales

1. To achieve the natural sea colours you need to grade various shades of blue and green with dry watercolour pencils, then wash over with a wet paintbrush.

2. The colour at the bottom of the background should be more intense. Use a wet paintbrush to pick up colour from the tip of your dark blue watercolour pencil and apply to the wet background.

3. Try colours such as green, blue, purple and yellow for the fish's body. Smoothly blend them together using dry watercolour pencils. Leave a highlight of white over the top of the fish's body.

SKETCHING WITH WATERCOLOUR PENCILS

4. With a dry, blue, sharpened pencil draw in the detail of the almond-shaped scales. Shade in the top of each scale so that they look raised. Add the detail to the eyes, mouth and fins with dry, green, blue and black pencils.

5. The colour of the coral can be created by grading shades of blue and green. Create the texture of the coral by shading light and then dark colours in a circular motion. For areas which are in the shade, intensify the colour with a layer of darker green and blue, dry watercolour pencils.

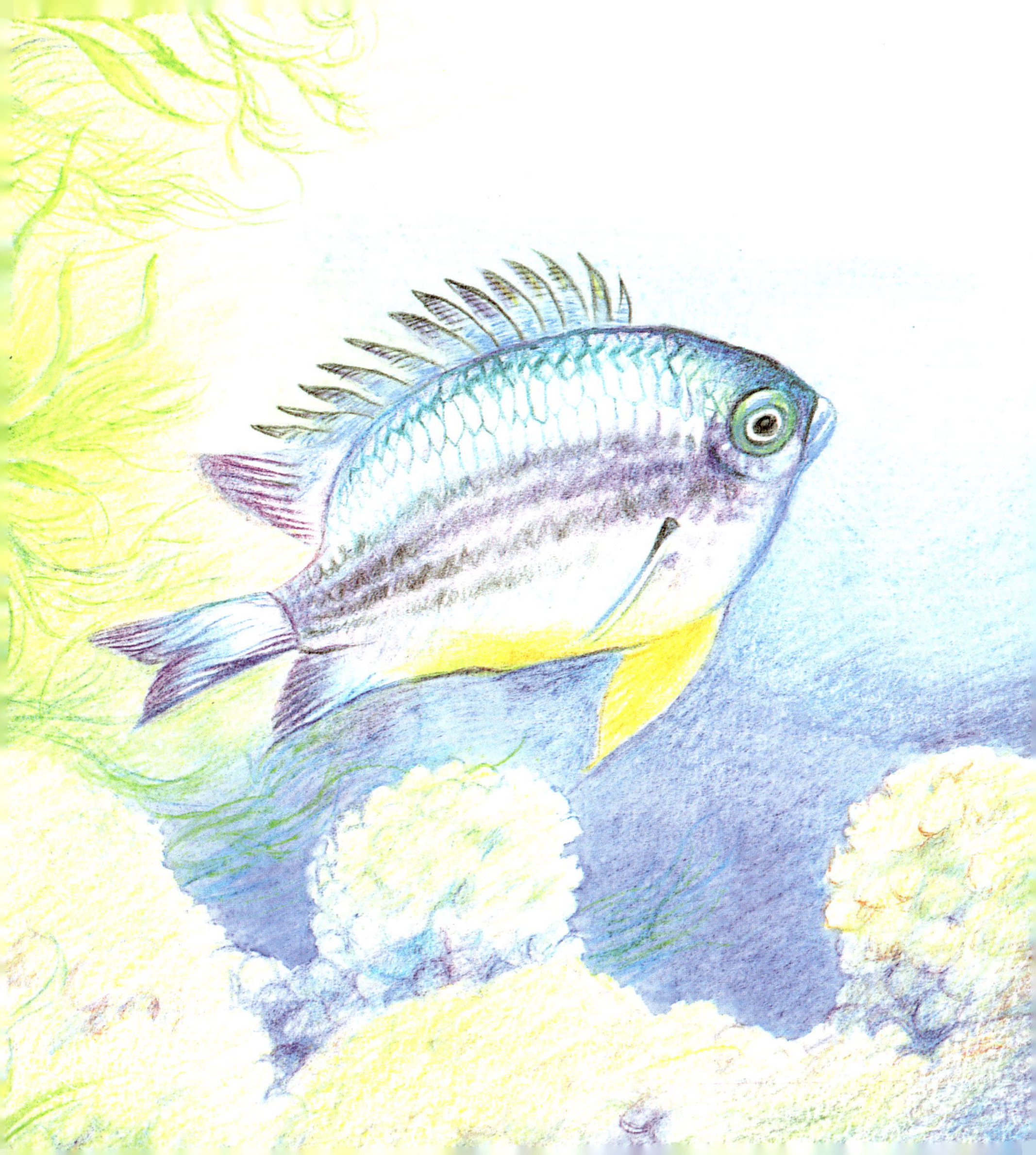

Colours you will need to mix for this project

30

Puppy and Kitten: Fur

1. *This long-haired kitten has very soft fur. Use dry, blunt watercolour pencils and short random strokes to create the yellow areas. Use a sharp, dry, blue pencil for the definition around the edges of the kitten's body to build up the sofa colour. Leave the white areas blank.*

2. *To sketch the puppy's short hair, shade in a yellow foundation with a dry watercolour pencil. Leave white spaces on the back of the dog to create the effect of light bouncing off the fur.*

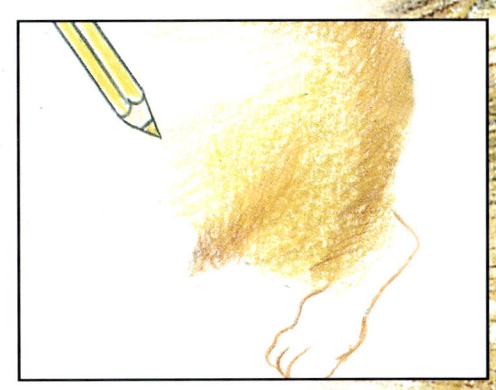

SKETCHING WITH WATERCOLOUR PENCILS

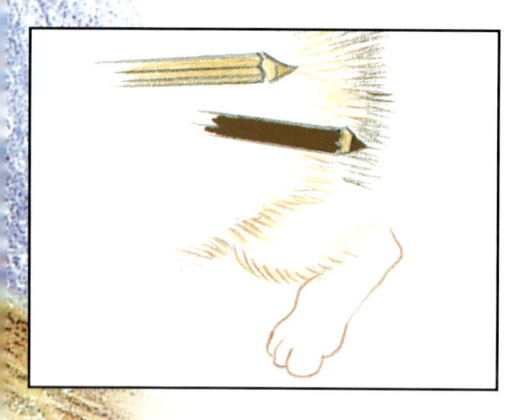

3. For the longer fur, apply short pencil strokes with a dry, brown, sharp pencil along the puppy's body. Use a black coloured pencil to help define the darker areas around the edges of the fur.

4. Colour the sofa (when you have finished drawing the animals) using a dry, blue pencil. Soften the colour using a wet paintbrush. When dry, add areas of shade with a wet watercolour pencil. Let it dry, then draw the indentation marks around the puppy's foot with a dark blue, dry watercolour pencil.

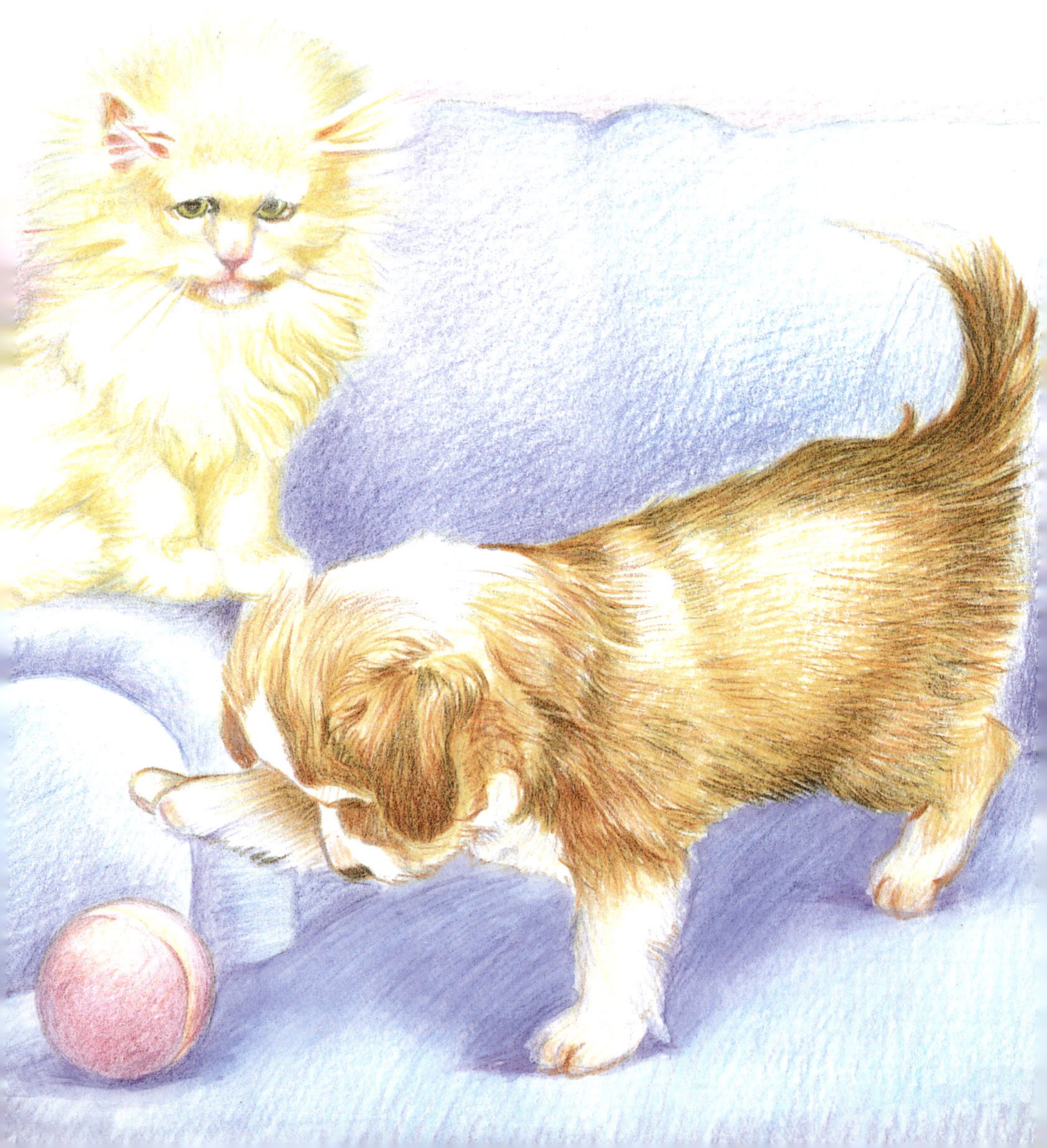

Colours you will need to mix for this project

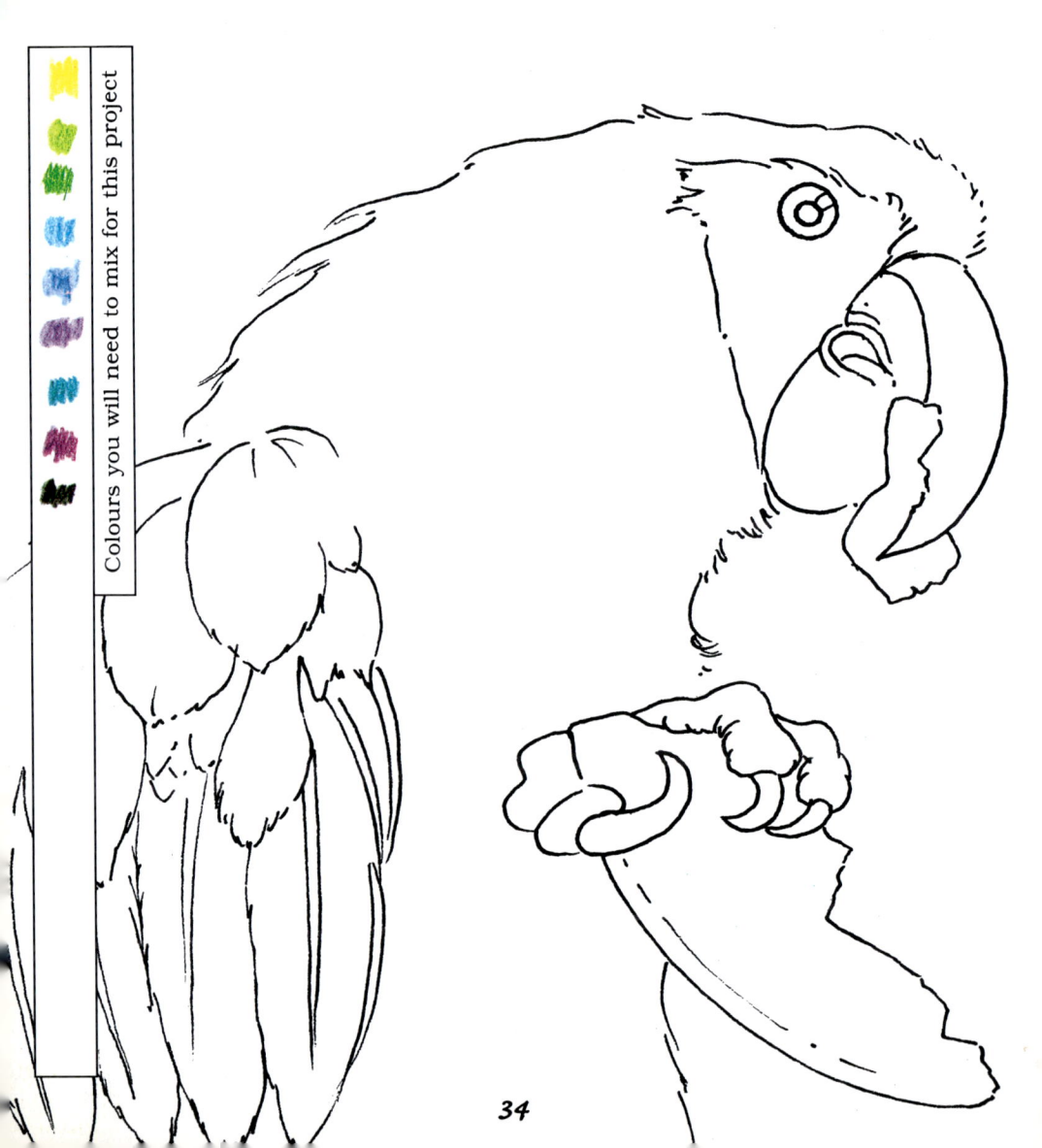

34

SKETCHING WITH WATERCOLOUR PENCILS

Parrot: Feathers

1. The technique of drawing feathers is similar to that of fur. Simply shade in the blue, yellow and green colours of the parrot's head and body with dry watercolour pencils, then smooth over with a wet paintbrush to soften the line work.

2. Add detail to the feathers using short pencil strokes with dry, sharp watercolour pencils in colours which match those used in step 1. Smooth feathers reflect highlights. Use a dry, white pencil to add highlights in the middle of each feather. Using such highlights will make your work look more 3-dimensional.

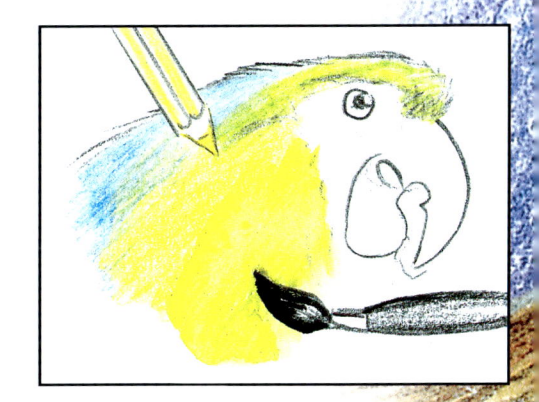

SKETCHING WITH WATERCOLOUR PENCILS

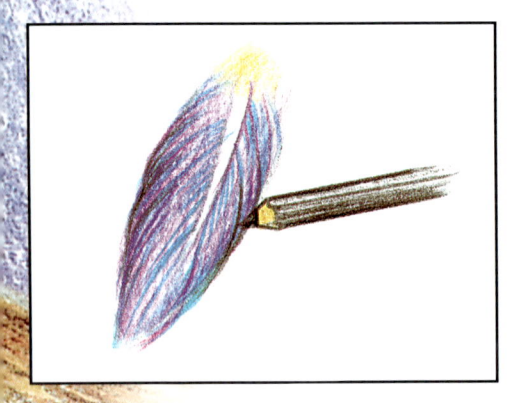

3. On the longer feathers, known as flight feathers, there is a lot of detailed line work. With a blue, dry watercolour pencil, draw smooth strokes from the centre of the feather to the sides. Shade in the tips and edges of the feathers with a black pencil.

4. Fill in the parrot's eyes, beak and claws with a dry, black watercolour pencil, then wash over with water, using your paintbrush. Make sure that you leave highlights of white in areas that are pronounced, such as the top of the beak and eyes.

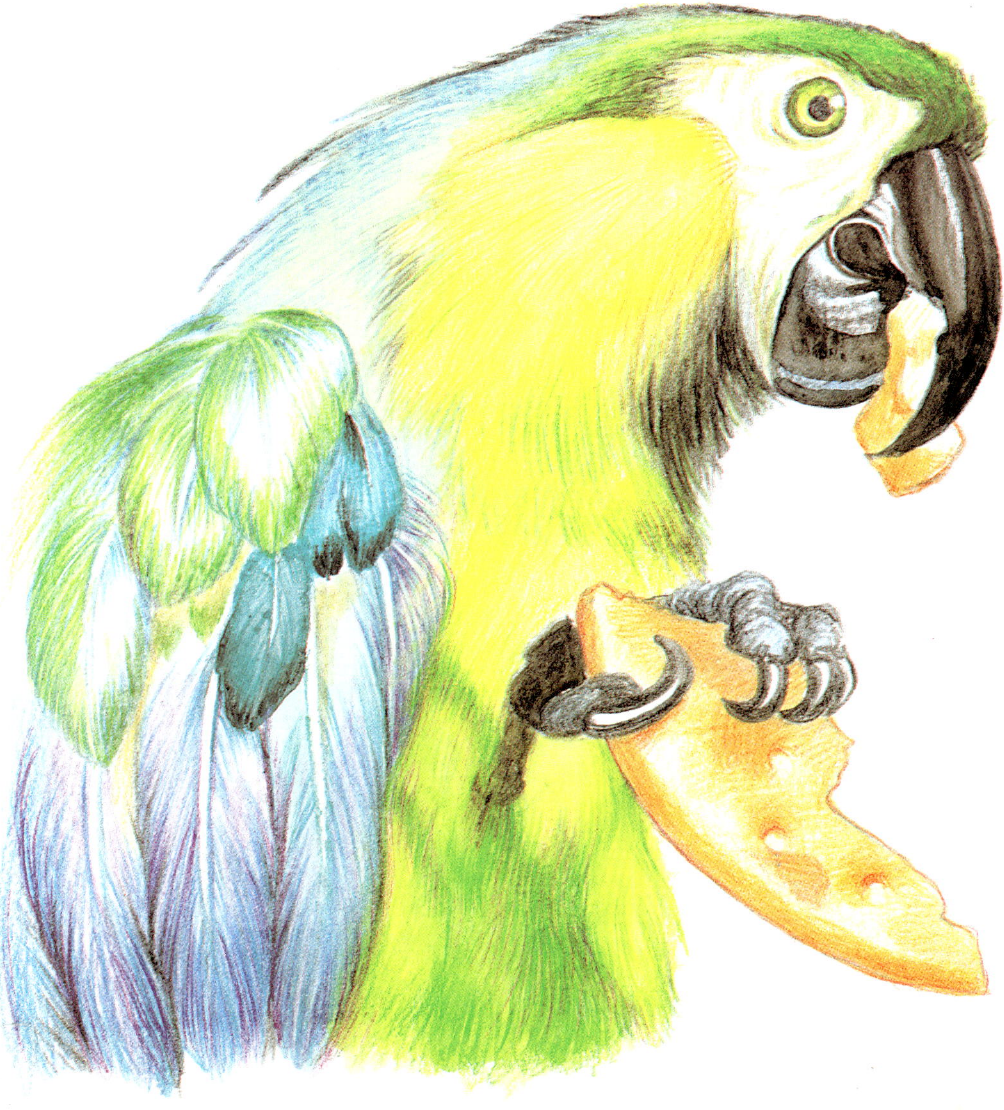

Colours you will need to mix for this project

38

Elephant: Skin Texture

1. Begin by lightly shading the elephant's entire face and body with a dry, yellow watercolour pencil and an ordinary pencil. Then paint over it with a wet paintbrush making sure no pencil marks can be seen. Allow to dry.

2. For the darker areas of the elephant's skin, crosshatch dry, blue grey and black pencils. Use a fine crosshatch for really dark areas and gentle crosshatching if the skin is lighter. Make sure that you allow the shading from step 1 to show through so that it highlights areas such as the head and top of the ears.

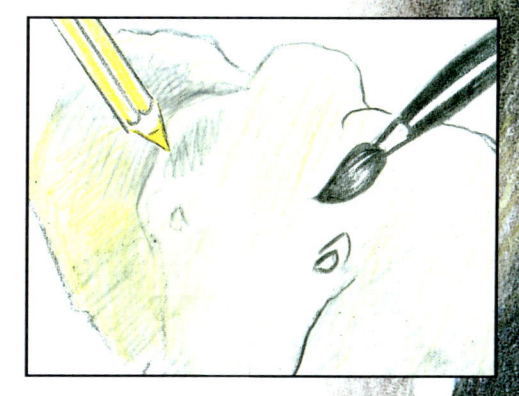

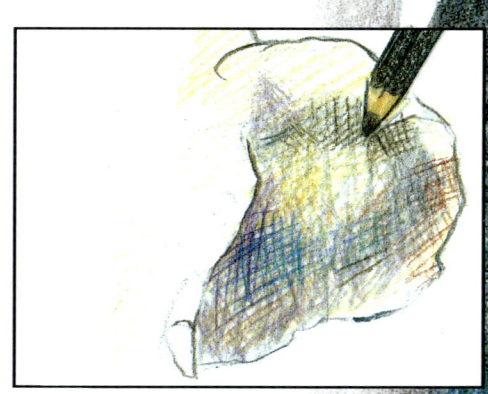

SKETCHING WITH WATERCOLOUR PENCILS

3. Now draw in the detail in areas where the elephant's skin is wrinkled, including the trunk and bottom of the ears. To do this, use a sharp, dry, black pencil. You can use an ordinary pencil to add some of the finer details.

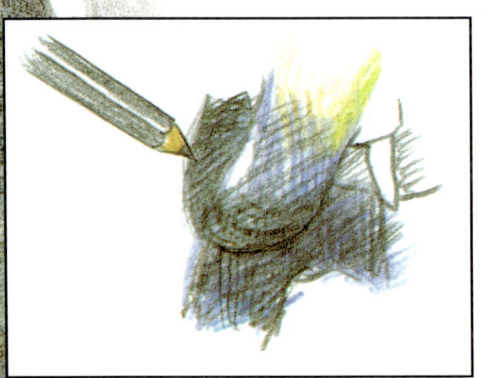

4. In areas that are cast in deep shadow, details become obscured. Avoid adding any details in these areas or you will ruin the shadow effect.

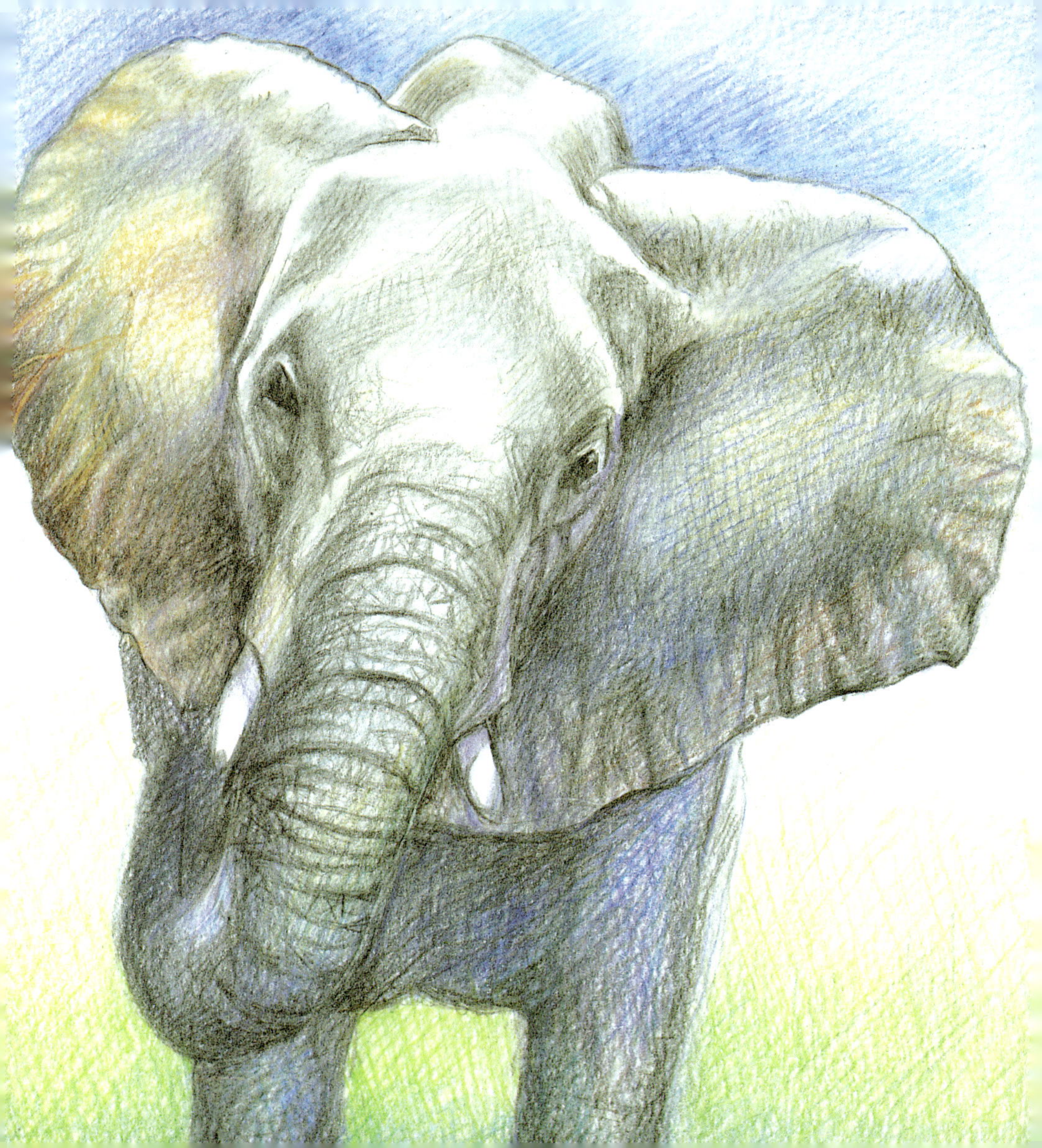

Colours you will need to mix for this project

42

Portraits: Skin Tones

Light Skin

1. First, use pale pink and yellow colours to shade in the shadows and contours of the face. Crosshatch colours in areas of shade to create more definition, leaving white highlighted areas on the hair, forehead, cheeks, nose, mouth and chin. Using sharp, dry watercolour pencils, build up red, beige and blue colour to accentuate darker areas of skin tone.

Dark Skin

2. For darker skin use strong pink and purple colours that are darker in tone than the colours used for lighter skin. Gradually build up these colours to create a foundation for the darker colours as you did for the light skin.

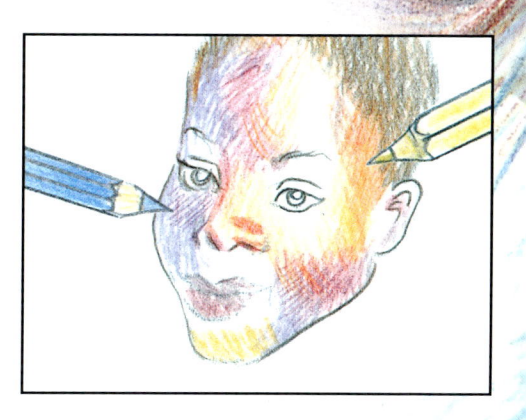

3. Next apply darker colours, such as brown, red and black to create a darker tone. Wet a black watercolour pencil and draw in the hair using the rolling technique explained on page 6. Soften the edges of the hair by adding wispy strokes, with a dry, black watercolour pencil.

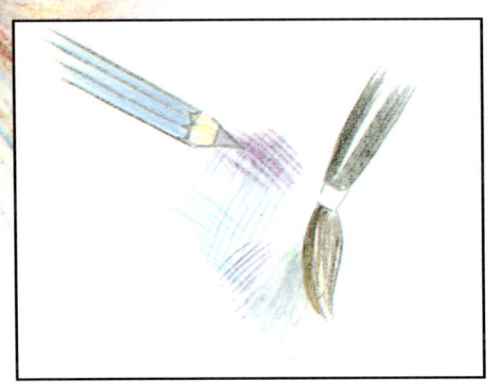

Clothes

4. Cross hatch various blue and mauve colours to achieve the creasing effects. To create more definition, use a wet paintbrush to paint over certain areas where natural shadows would form such as the shoulders and neck.

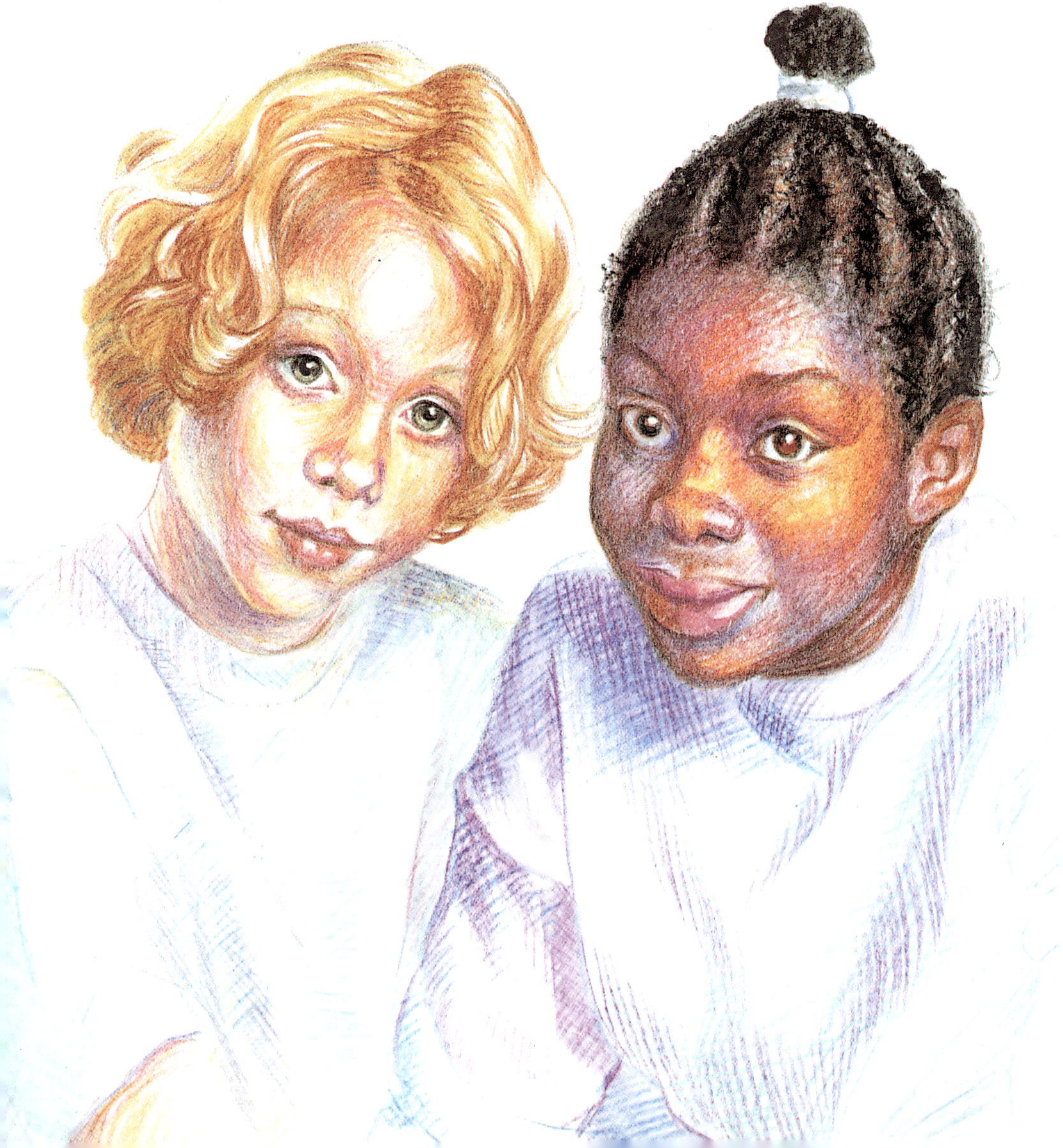

Poster Paints

Watercolour Tubes

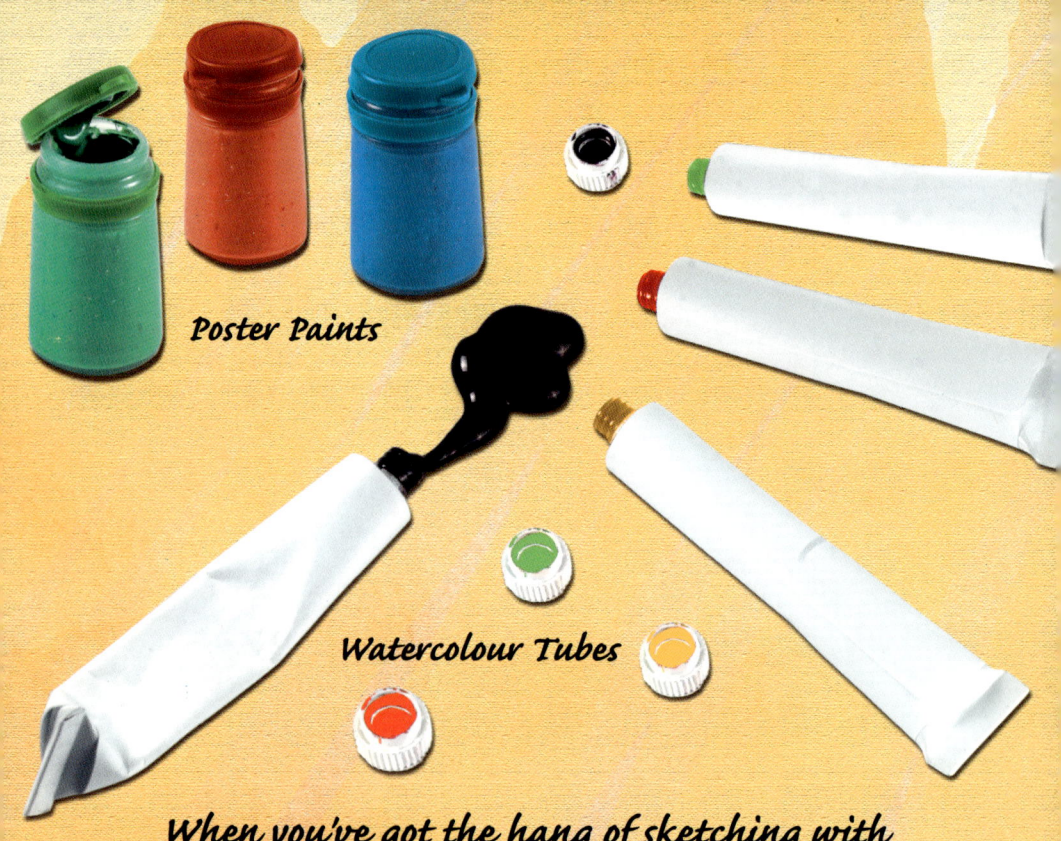

When you've got the hang of sketching with watercolour pencils, you could try out other water-soluble paints. Go to your local art and craft shop and see what different types of paint they have.

Poster paints come in bold, opaque colours which can be easily mixed.

There is a much wider range of colours available in tubes of watercolour paint, and they last much longer than the pencils.

Watercolour paints also come in watercolour pans. With these dry watercolours, you can achieve a more transparent effect.

You can use different sized brushes for new textures and shades. Use bigger brushes for larger areas of flat colour and smaller brushes to fill in fine details.

SKETCHING WITH WATERCOLOUR PENCILS

It takes a long time for watercolour pencils to run out, so you can practise the projects in this book as much as you like. You can buy watercolour pencils from any good art or craft shop if you do run out. When you have finished your pictures, you can frame them as a gift for someone or hang them on your wall. The watercolour pencils used in this book are all water-soluble. Any marks made with the pencils can be easily removed from clothes and surfaces.